THE 17 MISTAKES INVESTORS MAKE

DAVID BATCHELOR

Copyright © 2013 David Batchelor
All rights reserved.

ISBN: 1480262609
ISBN-13: 9781480262607

Seventeen common investing errors and how to avoid them

Contents

	Introduction 5
1.	Selecting investments without an asset allocation model 9
2.	Not doing the research 15
3.	Not understanding investment tax 21
4.	Not considering the impact of investments on your personal tax 27
5.	Believing cheap is good 33
6.	Believing expensive is good 37
7.	Buying investments with penalties 43
8.	Not knowing the real charges 47
9.	Not measuring performance 53
10.	Comparing apples with bananas (or a milk float with a Porsche) 57

11.	Not understanding risk	63
12.	Not measuring risk	71
13.	Sticking with bad investments	77
14.	Forgetting about inflation	83
15.	Following investment advice in the press	87
16.	Listening to the wrong people	93
17.	Not being on the ball	99
18.	Choosing the wrong adviser	113

Introduction

There is an old adage that says good decisions are made based on wisdom. That wisdom is a result of experience. Experience is often a result of bad decisions.

If the preceding is true, why is it that so many people make repeated mistakes when it comes to investing? Why is it that the same mistakes are made by so many, so often?

I cannot answer these questions, but I can say that most people don't seem to learn from the past. Most people seem to repeat past mistakes over and over again. They seem to do the same things over and over, and yet expect different results. One might think the situation would be different with wealthy people, but that's not the case. The

G9 Family Office Network is a company that works with the stupidly wealthy. How much is 'stupidly wealthy'? In their book, people with over £500m of investments. In the firm's research, in which 180 members of these extremely wealthy families were interviewed, they found that *all* of them had lost money when they invested with the disgraced former investment advisor Bernard Madoff. All of them! How many changed the way their wealth was managed following those losses? The answer is none. Not one of those 180 families did things any differently. It may be worth noting that none of those families actually generated the money that created their wealth—it was all inherited. If they had earned it, would they have done things differently? Probably.

Because most people do not learn from their own mistakes, or those of others, they are often unsuccessful when it comes to investing. This gives us a real advantage, because if we look at what the unsuccessful people do, we can make sure that we don't do the same.

Over the thirty years that I have worked in finance, I believe that I have been successful for two simple reasons. Firstly, I learn from my mistakes; this is a skill that most of us have but rarely use. More importantly, I learn from other people's mistakes.

In this short book I want to have set out the common mistakes made by investors so that you can avoid them. If you attend one of our free public education seminars, you will learn that we do not touch on these areas very much because we focus instead on what successful investors do, so that you can copy them. If you do not attend one of our events, I hope that in reading this short book you will find some activity or strategy that you are pursuing that can be put right. In this way, you will become more successful with your investments.

The seventeen common mistakes presented here are not in any particular order, although the first is the most important. Please read them all and ask yourself how many you are making. If you are making one, it should be easy to fix. But if you are making several, the negative impact can be exponential. Two plus two plus two equals six, but two multiplied by two multiplied by two equals eight. This is how mistakes in investing work: as the number of mistakes increases, the impact on your investments multiplies at an increasing rate. Therefore, you need to make changes to any negative practices as quickly as possible. There is no time to lose.

1

Selecting investments without an asset allocation model

INVESTORS MISTAKES

In 1986 there was a study completed by Brinson, Hood, and Beebower. The study was repeated in 1991 by Brinson, Singer, and Beebower. The study was intended to establish the most important influence on successful investing. In both studies the answer was the use of an asset allocation model.

What is an asset allocation model? Asset allocation is the process of selecting investments that complement rather than damage each other. The simplest example is investing in shares. If you invest in shares, their value will increase and decrease based on a number of different factors, but the point is, if you have shares that will both increase and decrease, you want to be:

1. investing in the shares that increase rather than decrease;

and

2. investing in a type of share that is increasing. The actual share is usually less important than the type of share.

For example, if you decide to buy shares in a bank, their value will tend to increase and decrease as other banks' shares rise and fall. Of course, this is not always the case, but it is so the vast majority of the time. Therefore, if you decide to purchase a bank's shares, your next share selections should probably not be for those of another bank. If you have shares in two banks, it can be great when prices go up, but when they go down your portfolio will be damaged very easily.

INVESTORS MISTAKES

This is a basic example, but it demonstrates the point. In the real world, investors tend to purchase a variety of shares. The question is, have you decided on the correct sectors for those shares, or are you just stock picking? Sometimes stock picking works, but it is rarely a successful strategy of the long term. Ideally, you would invest across diverse asset classes such as property, bonds, gilts, metals, commodities, etc. The absence of this asset mix is the biggest single factor that causes poor performance.

Not doing the research

INVESTORS MISTAKES

Do you remember the last time you bought a car? How much time did you spend before making the purchase? Probably you spent weeks looking at the options, buying car magazines, and checking out reviews on the web. Then you likely visited three or four showrooms, looking at the actual cars and taking each for a test drive or two, and then finally spent a week negotiating the deal.

When you purchased that car, how much did you spend? £15,000? £30,000? £70,000?

Now look at your investments. How much money did you invest, and how much research did you do?

Can you believe that some people buy shares in a company and don't even look at the company accounts? Worse still, can you believe that people buy shares without looking at the trading records to see if the company's own directors are buying or selling their shares? Ask yourself, would you invest in a company where the directors are selling their shares? It's best to mimic the actions of the directors; they will always know better than everyone else simply because they are close to what is happening in the company.

Have you ever purchased shares in a company without reviewing the accounts? If you did, why? Do you think Warren Buffett looks at the company accounts? If people buy shares without doing the research and they do well, it's luck. If the shares do poorly, it isn't bad luck, it's stupidity—not the people, their actions. When you attend one of our free public education seminars, you will find out the information you should review and consider when buying shares.

INVESTORS MISTAKES

We have seen people buy savings bonds without reading the small print, and without comparing the bond with the available alternatives.

If you are going to invest £50,000 and you are going to do it yourself, without advice, you must do the research. Spend at least the same amount of time doing the research that you would if you were buying a car.

Not understanding investment tax

I once spoke to a potential new client who had put money into an investment bond. When I asked why he chose the bond, he said, 'Because I don't pay any tax—it's tax-free.' In fact, these investments are not tax-free; the tax is deducted within the investment. However, the nature of the investment is that you don't see the tax. I explained this to the potential client, and he said, 'Oh, no, that's not right, it's tax-free. The man who sold it to me said so.' When I asked what they had charged him to place this investment, he replied, 'Nothing, there were no fees.'

Isn't that iInteresting! It was tax-free, and there were no fees—yet these bonds have tax deducted from them at source, and if you are a high-rate tax payer, on withdrawal you pay the difference between basic and higher-rate tax. On this type of bond, salespeople can earn from 3–7 percent when they sell a bond. Is that a no-fee, tax-free purchase? Or is it that the man just didn't know the real facts?

A penny of tax is a penny of money that you do not get. If you don't understand how the tax works, you will probably pay too much.

One of the fundamental mistakes investors make is not gaining a full understanding of the tax system and how it affects their investments. If you don't understand the taxation, how can you hope to minimise it?

Many people think that individual savings accounts (ISAs) are tax-free. This is not precisely the case. Interest from ISAs is tax-free, as are capital gains, but dividends are taxed at a rate of 10 percent.

INVESTORS MISTAKES

Before you make an investment decision, you must consider the tax implications and plan your taxation strategy accordingly. This, along with an asset allocation strategy, must be a part of your overall investment process.

Not considering the impact of investments on your personal tax

Do you have an accountant? If you do, do you meet annually to plan how to limit your tax in the coming year, or do they just file your return each year?

Tax is a complicated area, and most people do not really know how tax works and how it will be calculated or, more importantly, how the tax on investments affects the rest of your tax.

If you are over sixty-five, you receive an additional personal allowance. If your income goes up, you will lose all or part of the additional allowance as the income increases. This means that if you do better on your investments, the profits can be cancelled out by the decrease in your personal allowance, effectively an increase in tax.

Many investors don't know all the wrinkles in the system, and thus lose money. It's a mistake not to learn how investments are taxed, as noted in the preceding section, but it is just as bad to not understand how investment returns may affect your taxation in other ways.

There are many ways you can use the taxation system to your advantage to boost returns on investments. For example, higher-rate taxpayers can use certain pension investments to generate guaranteed returns of over 66 percent *in one year*. That's not a misprint—a return of 66 percent in one year. And yet most people do not take advantage of this strategy.

It seems like madness that people do not think through the impact of investments on their taxation. Failure to do so will always lead to a poorer financial situation.

Believing cheap is good

INVESTORS MISTAKES

We all like a good deal. The problem for many investors is that they confuse low price with good value.

Too many investors have bought into mistake number fifteen (see below), believing the press. The traditional media view is that financial products are too expensive, and in most cases it's true, but the problem comes when an investor doesn't know the real costs of an investment.

A 'cheap' investment is one for which you don't pay very much, but you get poor value for your money. If a fund manager is charging you 1 percent to run an investment, is their investment better than that of a 2 percent fund manager? Political parties have said in the past that if you pay more than 1 percent, then you are paying too much, but the real issue is how the investment has performed at the rate you pay. It's better to pay 2 percent and generate 6 percent returns than to pay 1 percent but earn only 3 percent returns. This is an obvious point, but one that many investors forget. They go for the cheaper options without looking at real performance (see mistake number nine).

The second lesson is that if it looks too good to be true, it probably is. There really is no such thing as a free lunch—if you go for a cheap lunch, it's probably not a very good choice, either.

6

Believing expensive is good

If cheap isn't good, what about expensive?

If you go into the supermarket and buy a good wine from its higher-quality section, you will pay twenty to thirty pounds a bottle. If you then go and buy a bottle for five pounds, is the thirty-pound bottle six times better? It depends on your tastes, but from my experience it's probably not. It may be better, but is it six times better?

This type of thinking leads to paying too much for investments. Paying too much is as bad as paying too little. In the review of the 180 wealthy families mentioned earlier, the average fee that they paid for their investments was astounding. You would have thought that with such large sums of money involved they would be paying lower fees, but this was definitely not the case. Indeed, attendees at the European summit for family investors reported that the amount that they were paying in investment fees was on average twice what they ought to have been paying.

So, how much should you pay? The answer is linked to the value you receive. Looking at fees alone can never tell you if an investment is a good deal. Evaluate the price in combination with what you get for it. And what you get must encompass two elements: service and performance. When considering service, you need to be working with someone with whom you are comfortable, someone who lets you know what's happening on a regular basis. You want someone who keeps in contact with you not to sell you things, but to keep you in the loop. Performance, too, can't be evaluated in isolation; it must be considered in relation to risk. Unless you know how much risk is at hand, you cannot assess whether the performance is acceptable.

At the bottom line, you need to be making more money than whoever runs the investment. If they are making more money than you, something is wrong.

Buying investments with penalties

7

Why do people buy investments that have withdrawal penalties? Perhaps the better question is, why do people sell investments with withdrawal penalties?

The answer to the latter question is obvious: to keep you in an investment. Why do they want you to keep the investment? Again, isn't the answer obvious? It's for one of two reasons: either to recoup the commission and sales costs they paid when selling you the investment, or to stop you from taking out your funds when it performs poorly.

There is no reason—at all, ever—to take on an investment that has an exit or encashment penalty. There are over 17,500 investments open to you in the UK. Among these you should be able to find a variety of investments that meet your asset allocation requirements and have no exit charges or penalties. Despite this, many, many investors end up with investments that have exit charges.

Many people selling investments will also sell you on the need to keep poorly performing investments. However, this strategy can best be defined as *rubbish*. In general, investments should be for the long term, but that's no reason to keep a poor investment. If an investment is not performing, change it. It's that simple. But if you have exit charges or encashment fees, it's hard to do this.

If you have investments with penalties or exit charges, you will always fall into the errors set out below in number seventeen. A simple rule to follow: never, ever, ever buy investments with exit charges.

8

Not knowing the real charges

If you don't know the charges associated with an investment, you can't make a real judgement about investing.

Looking back over the past twenty years, there has been a great deal of mis-selling. In virtually all cases of mis-selling, people who were sold a financial product didn't know what they were paying. They had no idea of the real cost.

When you consider buying a new investment, part of your decision process is based on the relative costs of an investment. But if you do not know the real costs, how can you compare investments? The answer is that you can't compare investments. And if you can't compare them, you can't make a reasonable decision.

While this may be evident, the majority of investors continue to invest without knowing the full cost of investing and how it will affect the performance of their investments. Rarely have I met someone who knew the bid/offer spread on an investment, for example. When you invest in shares, there is a difference between the buying and the selling prices. This is usually around 5 percent, but can be as high as 8 percent. This means an investment that has, say, a 6 percent bid/offer spread must earn 6 percent just to break even. And yet, in a random sampling of twenty-five investors, when asked what the bid/offer spread was on the last share they purchased, no one knew. Amazing, isn't it, to think that out of 25 people questioned, none of them knew the bid/offer spread on the last investment they purchased. They all knew that they had paid a dealing fee of twenty pounds or so, but not one knew the real cost of their investment.

Almost as important as this is who gets the fee you pay. This has a massive impact that most people never consider. For example, investors can buy from what are known as discount brokers. You'll often see these people advertising in the papers, usually with a pull-out leaflet, or even with a deal tied to the newspaper. These discount brokers explain how they allow you to invest more cheaply than if you bought an investment yourself or through an adviser, and in their literature they will often say how they receive no commission for setting up investments. If this is the case, ask yourself, how can they afford to print and advertise, pay their staff, and earn a crust if they do it for free? Remember mistake number five, believing cheap is good? Is there really something for nothing?

Many of these discount brokers genuinely do not receive a commission. However, the fund manager will charge a fee—

totally understandable, because someone's got to be paid for doing all the work. But here's the thing that you didn't know: the fund manager will usually give a percentage to the discount broker. What's wrong with that? Nothing in itself, but if you don't know about it, how can you make a judgement call?

In a circular I received with *The Times* recently, a discount broker, while not advising anyone to buy a fund, featured in very large writing its top five investments. What made them the top five? Well, it certainly wasn't because of performance. It certainly wasn't because of lower than normal charges. So what was it? Was it that these funds paid a large amount back to the broker?

If you knew that the brokers were receiving a larger payment on a fund, would you judge it differently?

9 Not measuring performance

INVESTORS **MISTAKES**

Whenever our company meets with a prospective client, the starting point is always to perform an investment audit. Unless you know where you are, you can't move forward. When we do this, we ask the potential new client, 'How well have you done so far?' How many can tell us exactly the percentage and pound amount they have earned on their investments so far that year, in the previous year, and since the investments have been in place? In the past twenty years, only two have been able to answer that question.

If you don't measure performance, then you will never know how well you are doing. If you don't know how well you are doing, you won't know what works or what doesn't.

If you are not measuring investment performance accurately, you will be repeating the mistakes of poor performers. All great and successful investors measure, measure, and measure again. And when they measure the investments they don't just measure performance, they also measure risk—but that's another story (see mistake twelve).

10

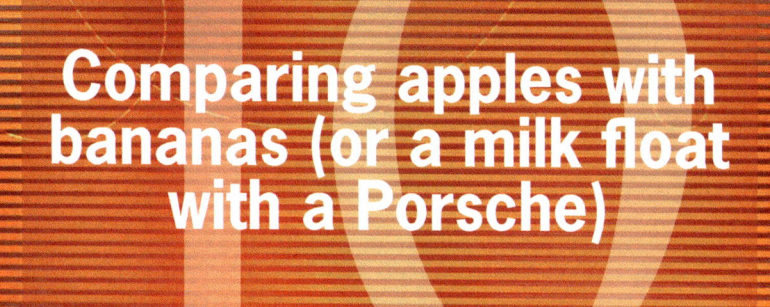

Comparing apples with bananas (or a milk float with a Porsche)

In the world of finance, people often seem to think that a milk float should travel as fast as a Porsche or that a Porsche should carry as much milk as a milk float. What on earth do I mean by this, and why is it so important? My rather bizarre example demonstrates how strange people's thinking processes can be when they look at investments, and it is this strange way of thinking that causes them to act erroneously.

Returning to the example above, if you purchased a milk float (for those of you who don't know what a milk float is, it's a small electric van that milkmen use to deliver milk in the early hours of the morning), you would purchase it for the purpose of delivering milk. It is specifically designed to carry a very heavy load, in a very quiet way, at relatively slow speeds. If you purchased a Porsche, you certainly would not want to use it to transport a thousand milk bottles. Firstly, because it would not be able to hold them, and secondly, because 'quiet' is quite the opposite of how a Porsche operates, and certainly not what Porsche drivers would like to do. Each of these vehicles is designed for a different purpose and so does different things well and different things badly. We all know this instinctively and thus don't compare one with another. However, in the world of finance, people tend not to think this way. People are often quite happy to compare one investment with another, with the objective of being able to say that one is better than the other.

Let's say you have decided that you want to retire and you want to invest your money to produce an income for your retirement. Looking for the best investment to hold to produce the income needed, you would start to compare investments. You might well compare an equity income fund with a fixed-interest investment. Both can be designed to produce income, and so on the face of it they can be compared. However, they are different in many ways. An equity income fund invests in shares that tend to produce high dividend levels. It is this dividend that's issued to produce the income. The capital will move up and down depending on the price of the shares, and the income will move up and down depending on the level of dividends. A fixed-interest investment is also designed to produce income. The income is produced by the 'coupon' of the investment and will be fixed for the lifetime of the investment. The value of the investment will fluctuate over time as demand for that type of investment varies. At the end of the term, the original investment would be returned.

These investments are totally different even though their objective is to do similar things. Despite their similar objectives, it would be wrong to compare them and say that one is better than the other. To say one is better is to compare the milk float and the Porsche. I often see this comparative thought process cause real problems for investors. Very often they will invest in an investment because they have compared it to another and it seems better. Usually, these mistakes occur when people compare investments based on performance only and do not take into account the underlying risk of the investment. This inevitably leads to people purchasing investments that have far too much risk, certainly more risk than they intend to carry. It is certainly advisable to compare similar types of investments, but this can be a dangerous game, and investors can all too often get it wrong.

11 Not understanding risk

What is risk? More importantly, how does it relate to investing?

I've always found it interesting that when people go on holiday and fly for the first time, they often decide it's time to make a will. Why is that? There is a greater chance of dying on the drive to the airport than dying in a plane crash, but people seldom can see that. And this is the problem with risk. Most people don't truly understand what it is or how they should think about it.

There are many risks associated with investing. I will not list all of them here, as I want to focus on what I think are the most important areas of risk that you should think about. Systemic risk, non-systemic risk, credit risk, and political risk are all important concepts to understand when you develop an investment portfolio. However, I believe that currency, liquidity, and operational risk are almost totally disregarded by the unsuccessful investor.

Currency risk

When you purchase different investments, the measurement of that investment is completed in currency—an obvious point, but one that people frequently forget when investing abroad. When we invest in another country—whether it's in property, in shares, or in commodities—we increase the overall risk significantly because we build in currency risk. Currency risk is where the value of the currency changes compared to pounds sterling. For example, if the exchange rate with the euro is 1:1.1, then for every pound you will receive 1.1 euros. If you invest in Europe, and the rate changes, the amount you make or lose will be amplified accordingly. This movement of currencies can have a bigger impact than the underlying performance of the investment itself. Successful investors use this to their advantage; unsuccessful investors don't even think about it.

Liquidity risk

This is a fundamental investment risk. Mistake number seven revolves around choosing investments that have exit penalties, a form of liquidity risk. If an investment is illiquid, it is difficult to get rid of, and when an investment is bad, you need to get rid of it. Many people fall into the mistake of buying illiquid investments. The problem is that they rarely see the problems that these illiquid investments cause until it's too late. A prime example of this is an investor who (against my advice) purchased wine as an investment. He was sold the wine over the telephone by a wine broker.

Every other month or so, the broker called to say how well the investments were doing and how much the wine had increased in value. And then, one month, the client wanted to take the money out because he needed it for his daughter's wedding. The problem was that when he needed the money, the wine magically became hard to sell. Although it was literally a liquid investment, it was not liquid. And as you can imagine, the investor had to accept a much lower price than the valuation to actually get his money out.

Operational risk

Sometimes things just go wrong. We can accept that when we invest, we should allow some margin for error in the decision-making process and the investment process itself. But when things go wrong operationally, it can completely derail our plans and strategies. I have a client who is keen on trading shares himself, and he has been reasonably successful. However, the trading account that he uses has a time delay, and for some reason whenever he wants to make an important and large trade, the site seems to slow down. This problem has cost him thousands over the years, and it seems to occur no matter the trading account he uses. It's all well and good 'paper trading' to experiment with your investment strategies, but it's not the same thing as trading with real money and dealing with real issues.

12

Not measuring risk

INVESTORS MISTAKES

In number nine above, we looked at the mistake of not measuring investment performance, or not measuring it properly. Measuring performance will bring you a step closer to doing well with your investments, but this is only half the story—the other side is measuring risk.

Mistake number eleven explained that most poor investors don't understand risk and explored some of the different types of risk. But if you don't measure the risk involved, there is no point in even knowing that it exists.

The most important type of risk to measure is volatility. This measures the size and speed and zig and zag of investments. Volatility is noted on most investments by a number. The higher the number, the higher the volatility.

Unless you know the volatility, you can't judge if the investment is a good deal.

For example, if the volatility of an investment is six and the rate of return is 10 percent, would you exchange it for an investment where the volatility is eight and returns are 15 percent? Clearly you might, taking on extra risk for higher potential return. But what if you then had the opportunity to choose an investment with a volatility of three and a return of 5 percent?

In this case you should switch, because the curve on volatility is exponential. By moving the volatility from six to three, you are not halving your risk, you are reducing it by about 75 percent. So, if you could reduce the risk by

75 percent but reduce the returns only by half, would you make the change? Of course you would.

If you don't measure the risk, you can't possibly make an informed investment decision.

13
Sticking with bad investments

INVESTORS MISTAKES

Surely if an investment was bad, you would change it, wouldn't you? The problem is that most people don't. By our estimations, less than 10 percent of people get rid of bad investments, and the issue is that the financial services sector works hard to stop investors from doing so.

If you had a financial adviser, and one of your investments fell in value, how many times have you been told, 'It's a long-term investment, you have to stick with it'? If you are like most of our clients, you will have heard this again and again, and 'sticking with it' is one of the biggest mistakes people ever make when it comes to investing.

If you are investing for the long term, of course investments will fluctuate over time. That's their very nature, but it doesn't mean you should cling to bad investments. If you have a bad investment, *get rid of it*. Get rid of it as soon as you can, and change it to…wait for it…a good investment!

Doesn't this just seem like common sense? Then why don't people do it? Well over 70 percent of the people that we meet for the first time are hanging onto bad investments, and they have had them for a long time.

So why do they keep them? There are three reasons:

- *You are told to keep them*. Very often you are urged to keep the investment by the person who sold it to you, because it's a 'long-term' investment. What you're not told is that the person who sold you the bad investment is getting a commission every single month that you keep it.

- *It's too expensive to change them.* Mistake number seven talks about choosing investments with penalties. If you have such an investment, you also have the incentive to keep it even when it's no longer appropriate. On top of that, the cost associated with buying new investments makes a change even less attractive.

- *You don't know that the investment is bad.* It's easy to tell when an investment is falling in value, but that doesn't necessarily mean it's bad; it might just be the way the sector is moving that day or that month. But when something goes up, can it still be a bad investment? In many cases, yes. For example, if you hold shares in a bank that go up by 5 percent, but the shares in other banks go up by 8 percent, you have a bad investment on your hands. But if you don't measure and don't review, you will never know.

14 Forgetting about inflation

Inflation is the wealth killer. Inflation will destroy your wealth more quickly than you realise because it is silent and creeps up on you without announcing its presence. Everyone knows that inflation can eat away at the value of your investments, but rarely do people think any further than that. If they did, they would not hold the investments that they do.

In the five years prior to the writing of this book, inflation averaged 3.9 percent. That doesn't mean inflation was at 3.9 percent for five years; it means it *averaged* 3.9 percent during that period. This was at a time when base rates were 0.8 percent on average. The best return you could get from a bank or building society was 2 percent. Any yet billions and billions of pounds were held in these accounts, all losing money. If interest rates were 2 percent, and inflation was

3.9 percent, that means you would have lost 1.9 percent each year.

The important point here is that the loss that you made is *compounded*. The averages are just averages, but the compounding effect is massive. Over time, the effect of the compounding of inflation means that for an average inflation rate of 3 percent, the actual rate is even higher than 3 percent.

The only real way to invest to protect against inflation is to invest in assets that grow faster than inflation increases. This sounds obvious, but it's clearly not. If it were, people would not be invested in deposit accounts when they produce a lower return than inflation.

Following investment advice in the press

INVESTORS MISTAKES

It's baffling to see how many people take advice from the newspapers or the media. For some reason, people seem to accept what the media say without question and often follow celebrity 'experts' without thinking things through. This behaviour, more often than not, leads to bad investment decisions.

You have likely realised by now that to be successful, you need to do the things that other people don't do. In fact, you usually need to be proactive and act long before others.

Imagine you are sitting on the M25 in a traffic jam. As you sit there, the lane to your right starts to move and continues to move as you sit there going nowhere. In frustration you pull into the moving lane. As you do this, what inevitably happens to the moving lane? You guessed it, it stops. As you sit there in the now stationary lane, what happens to the lane that you moved from? It moves, of course.

Why does this happen? The answer is simple. When you move into the new lane, so do many other people. The increase of people in the lane causes traffic to slow and stop. At the same time, the lane from which you moved speeds up because so many people have moved out of it.

This is exactly what happens in investing when you take the advice of the media. When you follow an investment recommendation given in the press, thousands of other people do the same. This has the effect of watering down the results, and often reverses them.

If you do the same as everyone else, you will get what everyone else gets, which is very little. To get ahead in investing, you need to do what everyone else isn't doing, and that will never be what the press says.

Two final points about the press. Have you ever seen a report on a topic in which you specialise? For example, if you are a surveyor, have you seen any reports or articles about surveying? If you are a doctor, have you ever read any reports about your speciality? If you have, how often has the report or article been correct? In my experience, rarely, if ever. Therefore, what makes you think financial and investment reporting will be correct?

Secondly, if you ever get to speak to someone from the public relations industry, ask them how much time they spend trying to get their clients into the press. When they do, is it for their clients' benefit, to push their clients' products or services? The answer will inevitably be yes. If you then speak to a journalist and ask how much of the news and reporting comes from press releases and PR, you will find the figure is staggeringly high.

16
Listening to the wrong people

INVESTORS MISTAKES

Where do you get your financial advice? Is it from an adviser? From the newspapers or TV? Or is it from your friends and family? If you are like most people, it will be a combination of these, which is fine. It's good to listen to lots of views. Two points to keep in mind that unsuccessful investors often fail to consider are the difference between opinion and fact, and evidence.

One of the mistakes that unsuccessful investors make when choosing an investment is that they listen to opinion only. An opinion is exactly that, an opinion. A fact, however, is something tangible that you can use to make investment decisions. The fact that a company has just purchased a new franchise is a fact. The profit projections for the company are opinions. Successful investors listen to both, but they focus on the facts and let the opinions take care of themselves.

Evidence is something that most investors overlook. There are many types of evidence that should be considered when making investments, but in this context the most important evidence of all is whether the person giving the advice is actually investing, too.

Over the years I have seen three types of advisers: there are those who sell investments but don't invest in them themselves; there are those who sell investments and invest in them, and do badly; and there are those who sell investments, invest in them, and do well. On balance, whom do you think you should listen to?

INVESTORS MISTAKES

When taking investment advice, I think it's important to ask the adviser what investments he or she has. It is also important to ask how well they have done. Have they done well because they are a smart salesperson, or is it because they are a good investor?

17

Not being on the ball

How often do you look at your investments? More importantly, how often do you review those investments to confirm that they are still investments you should keep?

Most investors tend to meet with their financial adviser every year, in some cases twice a year, to review their investments. The problem is that in this fast-moving world, this is not enough.

The question is, how often should you review your investments?

The answer is daily. 'Daily?' I hear you cry. Yes, daily. The world moves too fast not to check on things every day. If returns fall and you need to do something about it, it's no good checking the situation after six months and seeing how much you have lost. Investors must always be on the ball and take action quickly.

Above, I explained how important it is to get rid of poor investments, to measure performance, to measure volatility. Unfortunately, doing all these things is no good if you don't do it often enough. In the 'good old days,' it was sufficient to review your investments a few times a year, but that's no longer good enough. Investments must be monitored every day. That doesn't mean that you change them every day. Indeed, if you have the right investments in place, there should be no more than a couple of dozen changes a year to most portfolios. Unsuccessful investors just don't review their investments often enough and are not objective enough when they do review them.

The only way to make reviews and changes happen is to turn the action of reviewing your investments into a process. No matter what is going on in your world, the process needs to take place on a regular basis. Each time you review, work to answer the questions and accomplish the goals outlined below.

- *Does the portfolio need to be rebalanced?* We saw in number one above that the most significant characteristic affecting performance is asset allocation. However, the amount of each asset you hold will fall out of proportion on a regular basis as investments change. Rebalancing is the process of correcting that imbalance.

- *Lock in gains.* It is more important to avoid losing money than it is to make it. When an investment grows beyond what you expect, then you must lock in the unexpected gain. All investments rise and fall; the thing is to make sure that when an investment has gone up, you lock in the gain so as not to lose it if it goes down again.

- *Change investments.* When an investment isn't doing well, it needs to be changed. Part of the review process is to move in or out of investments as they fall into or out of your investment criteria. Consider which are to be amended or sold altogether because the investment no longer meets your requirements.

- *Save the tax.* In sections three and four above we talked about the importance of getting the tax right. One of the ways of doing this is through continual review of your investments. For many investments, capital gains tax is payable on the profits that you make. Each year you have a capital gains tax allowance, which you will lose if you don't use it. Therefore, when you make a gain you need to make sure you capitalise that gain (i.e., use it up by selling the investment), so that no tax is paid. If you retain the investment into taxation, then you will just be building up your portfolio to pay more of it to the taxman. Likewise, when you suffer a loss on an investment, it may be sensible to capitalise the investment to lock in the loss.

- *Do you need to use it?* There is a point to investing, and that's to be able to use your investments when you need them. One of the issues people sometimes encounter is that they need to access their investments at the wrong time from an investment point of view. They may need to take cash from an investment to help a child financially. (You can bet that the child will always need the help when the investment is down.) When you review your investments, do so with a view to when they may need to be spent. If you know you are going to need to spend, in the months beforehand, watch the investments so that you can draw them out when the time is right from an investment point of view.

So there we have it, seventeen common mistakes that unsuccessful investors make. There are certainly more, but this list encompasses the most 'popular.' If you can stop making these mistakes or avoid them altogether, then you will move into a much more successful investment world.

There is a flip side to all of this, of course, and that is doing the things that successful investors do. These will not simply be the converse of the seventeen mistakes, and if we look at successful investors we will find that their lists of best practices can vary widely because of the different ways to invest. That said, a good starting point is to ensure that you are not making these seventeen mistakes.

So where do you start?

The first step is to make the decision to do things differently, and then determine when you will make a change. If you have read this short book, you may not physically be in a place where you can make changes, even though you might be in the right place psychologically. And so decide when you will do something different. Will it be tomorrow? The weekend? The end of the month?

Then decide what changes you should make first. For most investors, I suggest looking at mistake number one regarding asset allocation. The problem with this mistake is that it's quite difficult to put right. It involves developing an asset allocation model, and then changing your investments to match it. The issue here is that many people do not have the knowledge or ability to develop an asset allocation model. In addition, your existing investments may not be set up in such a way that you can change them without incurring charges or costs. If you are in this group, you may want to look for someone who can help you. A good place to start the search is to look only at chartered financial advisers.

INVESTORS MISTAKES

Chartered financial advisers are advisers who have the highest level of qualification (fellows aside) and have been awarded this status by the Personal Finance Society.

If you are doing things yourself, I recommend focusing on the recommendations surrounding mistakes twelve (measuring risk), thirteen (dropping bad investments), and seventeen (being on the ball). These are probably the easiest and the cheapest to implement, and will have the biggest impact for the least amount of work. Of course, your investments will be different to virtually anyone else's, and without looking at them it is tough to tell you what to do, but from experience I know that dealing with these three areas will help you greatly.

The final piece of advice is to make sure that you stick with it. Investing is not a one-time activity; it involves time, effort, and focus. If you are managing your own investments, you must treat it like a job. You need to give it the time it deserves (and it will take time). You cannot expect great performance on a couple of hours a week. If you can't give your investments the time they require, then get some help. There are lots of good advisers out there who can assist you if that is what you need.

Choosing someone to help

I have been working in financial services since 1982, and in the thirty-plus years that I have been in this business I have seen great advisers and investors, and bad advisers and investors. I originally planned to feature eighteen mistakes that poor investors make, but I decided on seventeen because the eighteenth wasn't common to most poor investors. In reality, it is common to only about half the poor investors I see. Also, the eighteenth could be incorporated under mistake number sixteen, listening to the wrong people.

However, after having some of my own clients read the first draft of this small book, I decided after their comments to include mistake number eighteen as a bonus. We won't even increase the price of the book; it'll be a bonus just for you.

18

Choosing the wrong adviser

From what I can see, there are comparable numbers of good investors and poor investors regardless of their use of an adviser. Sometimes people happen to use the right adviser and get great results. Sometimes they use the wrong adviser and get poor results. Rarely, if ever, have I seen someone with the wrong adviser get good results. And so the question is, how do you avoid choosing the wrong adviser? But before you ask that question you need to ask yourself another: do I need an adviser at all?

If you are able to avoid all of the above mistakes yourself, then you might not need an adviser. If you have the time to do the proper research on your investments, then you might not need an adviser. If you understand taxation and how it affects your investments, you might not need an adviser. The need for an adviser is not black or white; it depends on the investor. But if you cannot address all of the investing mistakes yourself, you stand very little chance of doing all the things you need to do to be successful, and in that case you should look to an adviser for help.

Choosing an adviser

If you have determined that you need an adviser to help you, consider the following when making your choice:

- *Work only with people who don't get paid a commission.* By this I mean work only with people to whom you actually write a cheque for their fee. If you do not pay them a fee directly, you will not know exactly how or how much they get paid, and if you don't know what they get paid, you cannot be sure that their advice is impartial. *Never* work with anyone who is paid from investment deductions. If you do, you will never be able to tell why your adviser recommends one investment over another.

- *Work only with people who invest in what they are recommending.* While there may be some investments that are not appropriate to everyone, I am always suspicious of people who don't invest in what they recommend.

- *Make sure they are sufficiently qualified.* Following changes implemented by the Financial Services Authority in January 2013, all advisers need to be qualified to a certain standard. However, in my opinion, this standard is still relatively low. Therefore, I recommend that you only use advisers who are qualified to 'chartered' level, or, at the very least, 'certified' level.

- *Look for a personal relationship.* Investing is a long-term commitment. If you cannot build a relationship with the adviser and his or her team, then things will break down in the long term. Therefore, you need to be comfortable with the adviser and actually feel comfortable in their presence. Never work with someone you don't like, however good their results or qualifications may be.

- *Look for someone with a great team.* No one can do it all, and no one can know it all. For someone to be a great adviser, they must delegate activities that do not directly support that function. If an adviser has only one or two people working with them, they may not be able to provide the level of support that they are offering.

- *Look at their office.* This was a piece of advice passed to me by my grandfather. He said you can tell a lot about a man from the way he dresses, and I believe the same is true about someone's office. We have all been in the stunning office where we ask, 'Are our fees high because of the cost of all this?' Likewise, we have all been to offices that certainly wouldn't inspire confidence. When you visit someone's office you will get a better feel for them and how they work.

DAVID BATCHELOR

I am sure there are many other issues that you will consider important, and you should add these to your list, but if you use my list as a starting point you will not go far wrong.

About The Wills & Trusts Group and David Batchelor

The Wills & Trusts Group was founded by David Batchelor in 1992 after he received a £9,000 inheritance from his grandmother. The business has grown since then and now has its head office in Thame, Oxfordshire.

The company deals with client investments, investments through the Court of Protection, and investments for other financial advisers, and it has produced significant returns at low risk since the development of The Advanced Investment Strategy in 1995. In 2012 the company was awarded chartered status.

The company sponsors over thirty public education seminars each year, covering subjects such as wills, reviews, investments, pensions, and long-term care planning. The seminars are part of the group's strategy to help people become better educated in the world of financial services.

David Batchelor is a former president of the Life Insurance Association, and led the merger of the LIA and the Society of Financial Advisers to create the Personal Finance Society, which is now the largest financial services professional body in the UK. David is qualified to certified adviser level and is a chartered financial adviser.